FRENCH'S STANDARD DRAMA.

The Acting Edition.

No. CCIX.

# AMERICANS IN PARIS;

OR,

# A GAME OF DOMINOES.

A Comedy, in Two Acts.

TO WHICH ARE ADDED

A description of the Costume—Cast of the Characters—Entrances and Exits—Relative Positions of the Performers on the Stage, and the whole of the Stage Business.

AS PERFORMED AT WALLACK'S THEATRE.



NEW YORK:

SAMUEL FRENCH,

122 NASSAU STREET, (UP STAIRS.)

## Cast of the Characters.—[AMERICANS IN PARIS.]

| | *Wallack's*, 1858 |
|---|---|
| *Arthur Morris* | Mr. Lester |
| *Doctor Botherer* | Mr. Blake |
| *Monsieur Lamouret* | Mr. Davenport |
| *Colonel De Sabres* | Mr. Grosvenor |
| *Monsieur De Lucenay* | Mr. Tree |
| *Baptiste* | Mr. Jeffries |
| *Joseph* | Mr. Parsloe |
| *Amelia*, wife of Morris | Mr. Hoey |
| *Annie*, wife of Dr. Botherer | Miss Gannon |

**Costume.**—Present Day.

Time in Representation—one hour and thirty minutes.

## STAGE DIRECTIONS.

L. means *First Entrance, Left.* R. *First Entrance, Right.* S. E. L. *Second Entrance, Left.* S. E. R. *Second Entrance, Right.* U. E. L. *Upper Entrance, Left.* U. E. R. *Upper Entrance, Right.* C. *Centre.* L. C. *Left Centre.* R. C. *Right of Centre.* T. E. L. *Third Entrance, Left.* T. E. R. *Third Entrance, Right.* C. D. *Centre Door.* D. R. *Door Right.* D. L. *Door Left.* U. D. L. *Upper Door, Left.* U. D. R. *Upper Door, Right.*

*** The reader is supposed to be on the Stage, facing the Audience.

# AMERICANS IN PARIS.

## ACT I.

SCENE I.—*Parlor in Mr. Morris' House.*

*Enter* JOSEPH *and* LAMOURET, L. C.

*Jos.* Monsier Lamouret.

*Lam.* [*Comnig sn.*] Is Madame Morris at home?

*Jos.* Yes, sir; she has not yet left the table.

*Lam.* M. Morris, then, is dining out?

*Jos.* I suppose so, sir. Madame waited until seven o'clock.

*Lam.* Ha! ha! [*Aside.*] Then he didn't tell her. [*Aloud.*] Joseph.

*Jos.* [*Going out, but stopping at the door.*] Sir.

*Lam.* I think I didn't give you your Christmas box the other day.

*Jos.* Oh, sir, that doesn't signify.

*Lam.* I fogot it, my man. But [*puts his hand in his pocket*] you won't lose by that. I say, Joseph; you like your place, I suppose?

*Jos.* I've been in the family, sir, ever since they came to Paris.

*Lam.* That's a good old-fashioned reason, but now-a-days you might have a better. I suppose they give you good wages?

*Jos.* Capital.

*Lam.* Then of course you like your place; and you must be anxious to have things go on smoothly, to have your master and mistress on the best terms with one another, and well, sometimes, *I have thought* that—hey? [*Plays with his purse.*

*Jos.* [*Stupidly.*] I don't know, sir.

*Lam.* Oh. you know what I mean. You see, I am so intimate with both Madame and Monsieur Morris, and they are here so far from home; and—and—a— What do you think of things among you down stairs?

*Jos.* Nothing but what is right, sir.

*Lam.* They never say sharp things to one another at table, I hope?

*Jos.* I never listen, sir; and they speak English when they are alone.

*Lam.* Ah, yes! But then the *tone*, you know—it isn't the words that signify. When a woman chooses to say provoking things, she may talk Chinese if she like—a man can't help understanding her.

*Jos.* I never watch them, sir, when they are talking.

*Lam.* [*Aside, putting back his purse.*] Then what the devil *does* he do?

*Jos.* [*Smiling.*] I will let Madame know that Monsieur is here. [*Exit*, R.

*Lam.* There's an astute servant! The fellow doesn't earn his salt, and it was devilish lucky I didn't begin by giving him six francs. Never mind. I'll bet that something is wrong in the house. Not a bad job, either. Madame Morris is charming—all these New York women are. I dare say I should have been fool enough to marry her myself, if I hadn't been so afraid of sea-sickness that I wouldn't accept Morris' invitation to visit him over yonder among his Camanches and his Mississippies. However, it's better late than never—perhaps better late than *ever*. If I had married her she might have disgraced herself by taking a fancy to Morris. Now she is married to Morris she may aspire to a fancy for me. In fact, I strongly suspect she is beginning to look that way already, and only needs a little encouragement. Decidedly, it is my duty as a Frenchman and a gentleman to give her a lift.

*Enter* AMELIA, R. H., *and* JOSEPH, *bringing a light, which he places on the mantle, and begins to poke the fire.*

*Ame.* [*Graciously.*] Ah! good evening, my dear Monsieur Lamouret. Why did you not come in a little sooner, that I might have had the pleasure of your company at dinner? I was alone.

*Lam.* [*With a conceited air.*] A tete-a-tete! Ah, Madame! there would have been half-a-dozen suicides to-morrow if I had been so fortunate.

*Ame.* [*Aside.*] What a bore he is! [*Aloud.*] Joseph, did Monsieur Morris tell you when he went out that he shouldn't come in to dinner?

*Jos.* No, Madame.

*Ame.* Nor that he should come home late?

*Jos.* He left no message at all, Madame.

*Ame.* It's very singular. [JOSEPH *goes out*, C. *She looks at the time-piece, and says, aside,*] Eight o'clock!

*Lam.* [*Aside.*] There's something wrong. [*Aloud.*] Are you uneasy, Madame? No doubt Morris has been kept down town by his business.

*Ame.* So I suppose. One can't always get away from one's office, and I believe there is a steamer from Havre to-morrow.

*Lam*, Ah! It's a pity, though, that one shouldn't give one's wife a word of notice. [L. *at mantle.*

*Ame.* Oh! one can't think of everything.

*Lam.* And husbands never think of anything.

*Ame.* You don't seem to have a good opinion of husbands.

*Lam.* [*Smiling.*] Not I! They are abominable creatures—I have the worst possible opinion of them.

*Ame.* And the best possible opinion of yourself, I suppose.

*Lam.* Undoubtedly; and I don't marry because I don't wish to lose my own respect.

*Ame.* Well, I dare say you are right, as a Frenchman particularly; but I assure you there *are* some good husbands in the world.

*Lam.* Really!

*Ame.* Mine, for instance.

*Lam.* Oh, heaven forbid I should question *that!* He is my dearest friend; and then [*bowing in an overwhelming manner*] he has every possible excuse for declaring himself an exception to the rule.

*Ame.* Of course he has to devote himself to business. Life in Paris is so expensive; and then he must think of the children. But he suffers more than I do from the restraint which his occupation imposes on our intercourse. And we have been so very happy always; and with all your art, you Parisians have never succeeded in turning his head. We live as quietly here, almost, as in New York.

*Lam.* That domestic Paradise! Ah, Madame! how frivolous an existence here must seem to you, accustomed, as you were, to the sobriety and economy of that Puritanic capital in which you were born!

*Ame.* [*Simply.*] I see but little of it, and my husband is so much engaged.

*Lam.* [*Aside.*] I am wrong—there is nothing the matter.

*Ame.* But, pray, take a chair. [LAMOURET *is about to sit down*—MRS. M. *listens.*] Hark, a carriage! perhaps it is M. Morris.

[*She opens the window and looks out.*

*Lam.* She certainly *is uneasy;* she certainly *has* a presentiment. Lamouret, my boy, you are in the right track—attention! [AMELIA *slams the window to.*] All right! she is perfectly savage. [*She sits down, and snatches up her embroidery.*] Splendid! they'll have a glorious blow-up this night!

*Ame.* [*Composing herself.*] What have you been about this week? Any balls? Anything new at the theatres?

*Lam.* Oh! I dare say. But I am so weary of all that kind of thing. The heart is left unsatisfied——

*Ame.* [*Interrupting him.*] I went to the last concert.

*Lam.* With Morris?

*Ame.* [*Vexed.*] No! With Doctor Botherer and his wife.

*Lam.* Ah! the inseparables—the Siamese couple. There is a model dove cot.

*Ame.* [*A little provoked.*] Yes, certainly; you never do see one of them without the other. They carry it so far that the doctor refused to be my boy's *godfather* with any other *godmother* but his wife.

*Lam.* What scrupulous fidelity! It's really quite discouraging.

*Ame.* Discouraging! to whom?

*Lam.* To all the adorers of Madame Botherer.

*Ame.* There's you French!

*Enter* JOSEPH, C., *throwing open the door.*

*Jos.* Madame Botherer.

*Lam.* [*Rising.*] Ah! Madame Botherer.

*Ame.* Show her in. [*Aside.*] If she will only take this simpleton away!

*Enter* ANNIE, C.

*Annie.* Good day, my dear. [*Seeing* LAMOURET.] Ah! I beg your pardon; I interrupt you.

*Ame.* Not at all. This is Monsieur Lamouret, an old friend of my husband. [LAMOURET *and* ANNIE *exchange salutes.*

*Annie.* The doctor has just gone out to visit a patient, and I took advantage of his absence to come down and ask a favor of you. I thought you were alone.

*Lam.* [*Taking up his hat.*] Secrets! then permit me to bid you good day.

*Ame.* What, you are not going?

*Annie.* Pray don't let me drive you away.

*Lam.* By no manner of means. But I just remember an engagement. I will come back a little later, in the hope of finding Morris at home.

*Ame.* You may be sure he won't be long out.

*Lam.* [*Aside.*] If I could only find out where my gay friend has been dining. I'll just reconnoitre the street as far as the *Café Anglaise.* [*Aloud.*] Ladies, your servant. [*Exit.*

*Ame.* [*Crosses,* L.] Thank heaven, he has gone. I am infinitely obliged to you, my dear Madame.

*Annie.* [*Crosses,* R.] What, for driving off your adorer?

*Ame.* For ridding me of a tedious creature, who can't utter three consecutive words of common sense. [*Crosses,* L.

*Annie.* Well, my dear, if I have done you so good a turn, you surely will do me another?

*Ame.* With all my heart. But what is it?

*Annie.* Just to put on a blue domino that I have prepared, all ready for you, and go with myself and Madame de Lucenay, and Madame Giraud, at midnight, to the masked ball at the opera.

*Ame.* My dear Madame Botherer, what on earth can you be thinking of?

*Annie.* Why, my dear child, I don't mean any sort of harm; I only want to amuse myself a little, and I thought, as you were a stranger, you would like to see the ball as well as me; and Monsieur Morris, I am sure, won't object when he comes home, even if you ask him.

*Ame.* I should never dare to think of asking him such a question. Why, isn't it frightfully improper and imprudent, and——

*Annie.* [*Sits.*] And entertaining. Yes, my love, it is *excessively* entertaining, everybody declares, and I shall never have such a chance again in all my life; for to-night the doctor is to go to the hospital at twelve o'clock, and for the first time since my marriage, I shall be left alone for three or four hours of the night.

*Ame* [*Interrupting.*] And I wish with all my heart that I could say as much, for Mr. Morris is continually leaving me alone.

*Annie.* Now don't be troubled about that, my child. If you knew what it is to be bored to death by a devoted spouse, as I am! It's very odd. My husband, I suppose, treats me like an American, and yours treats you like a Frenchman, and we are neither of us satisfied. But never mind that. We didn't make the world, and we can't mind it, and I don't find any fault with anybody. And you *must* come to the ball to-night.

*Ame.* Indeed, I assure you, it is altogether out of the question, and I should never think of—— And where in the world can Mr. Morris be? [*Walks about, very much agitated.*

*Annie.* Now, my dear, do compose yourself. If you fall into such an excitement, you will quite get beside yourself. And when Mr. Morris *does* come home, you will just drive him out again with a flurry of questions. He may hate to be questioned, and maybe he is perfectly sick with your tears, even hate to be cried at; and, my dear, take my advice: Change your tactics; wear a pleasant and smiling face, and show by your manner that you trust and confide, and thus make his home so happy that he will always be glad to return to it.

*Enter* JOSEPH, *who throws open the door.*

*Jos.* Mr. Morris.

*Annie.* [*Hurriedly.*] We will talk about this another time. [*Sits,* R.

*Enter* MORRIS.

*Mor.* Ah, my dearest Amelia! how excessively annoying. [*Seeing* ANNIE.] Ah, Madame! I am delighted to see you. I hope you have been keeping my wife company during all this time that I have been kept away from her by a confounded bore—a man that I met.

*Ame.* Ah! a man that you met! Where did you dine, then?

*Mor.* We dined—we dined—at the Cafe.

*Ame.* [*Looking at him suspiciously.*] And you dined pretty well, too, if I am to judge by your eyes.

*Mor.* Good, that! my dear. Judge by my eyes! Why, so far from that, we had the simplest dinner possible—quite a parson's dinner. A mutton chop, some codfish, and just a bottle of claret between us. Unless you see the codfish in my eyes, my dear, I am sure I don't know what you do see there. [*Aside.*] Damn that champagne! Do what we like, it always will show; it's as bad as segars.

*Ame.* And pray, with whom did you eat this self-denying dinner?

*Mor.* With whom! Oh, my dear, if I should tell you you wouldn't know.

*Ame.* [*Petulantly.*] Never mind. Who was he?

*Mor.* Well, then, he was—he was a merchant, a merchant of Buffalo, suddenly called home from a town in Palestine, by the news of the panic and the pressure in Brazil, and who want's some accommodation. A Mr.—[*hesitatingly*]—a Mr.—Stiffelbackenhoven.

*Ame.* What a name! One would really suppose you had cooked t up.

*Mor.* Ha, ha! very fine—very funny indeed. First you see a codfish in my eyes, and then you charge me with cooking up names. I beg leave to ask, in the most respectful manner, whether you distinctly object to that gentleman from Buffalo bearing the name Stiffelbackenhoven?

*Annie* [*Laughing.*] Ha, ha! it certainly is a very droll name.

*Mor.* [*Laughing, too.*] No, do you think so? It's a New York name

—a New York name. My wife ought ,o know it. A very respectable name; a name of Dutch origin, like many other things in New York. *Stiffelbackenhoven!*

*Ame.* Very well; and where have you been all day long?

*Mor.* Eh! more questions! [*Addresses* ANNIE.] Would you believe it, Madame, I can never go in or out of the house without undergoing a cross-examination. Where are you going? Where have you been? What have you seen? And do you know, questions craze me, vex me, turn me inside out, swell np my head as big as three. [*Addaesses* AMELIA.] Well, Madame, I've been at the exchange. Are you satisfied with that? [*Goes to fire-place.*

*Annie.* Of course he has. [*In a low voice to* AMELIA.] Go and speak to him.

*Ame.* [*Going up.*] And you've only been at the exchange?

*Mor.* Why, certainly.

*Ame.* Are you sure?

*Mor.* The whole blessed long day. Are you still out of sorts?

*Ame.* [*Putting out her hand.*] No, I am not.

*Mor.* [*Kissing her hand.*] So much the better. I should have been sorry to quit you out of temper.

*Ame.* Quit me! You are not going out again?

*Mor.* Oh! not immediately; a quarter of an hour or twenty minutes, or so. I have an engagement; some bills to draw to-night for—for——

*Ame.* For Mr. Stiffleblaxenhuffen, perhaps.

*Mor.* Exactly; he leaves in the steamer from Havre to-morrow.

*Ame.* And I am to stay here alone, am I? I shall die of ennui. But what does that matter? Once more or less. [*Crosses to* L.

*Mor.* [*Impatiently.*] One would really suppose I wanted to go out. [*Aside.*] Why the devil did I make such a fool of myself as to come in?

*Annie.* [*Aside to* AMELIA.] Ah, my dear! would to heaven my Botherer knew a Stifflebackenhoven.

*Both.* [*On the landing.*] Very well, Joseph; I don't need, by Jove, to be announced. [*Entering.*] Friends, your humble slave.

[AMELIA *bows.*

*Mor.* [*Presses his hand.*] Good evening, doctor.

*Annie.* What, back already! You didn't stay long with your two patients.

*Both.* Why should I? Nothing the matter with No. 1; No. 2 dead, stone dead; ninety-five years of age; no fault of mine that *he* died.

*Mor.* [*Gaily.*] Ah, doctor! it is the exception that proves the rule.

[*Sits down by the fire-place.*

*Both.* Joker! [*To* ANNIE.] When I came in, they said you were here; and so here am I.

*Annie.* [*Aside.*] Of course.

*Both.* Allow me to embrace my wife. [*Kisses her.*] A way I have—I never enter or leave my house without this formality. I have borrowed the custom from my father, who never abandoned it for more than half a century. I trust to follow his example.

*Annie.* [*Aside and smiling.*] There is a pleasant perspective.

*Both.* [*To* MORRIS.] Now, then, my dear Mr. Morris, what a bit of quicksilver you are. What do you do? Where do you go? I never stumble on you at your office or at the exchange.

*Mor.* [*Disturbed.*] Why, did you go there to-day?

*Both.* Three times, to ask you about those Erie bonds of mine Couldn't find you; supposed you were afraid to face an indignant Europe. [*Laughing.*

*Mor.* You didn't look for me, then.

*Ame.* No, you didn't look for him; he was there all day long.

*Mor.* All day long.

*Both.* Allow me. At two o'clock I saw you in the Rue Jombert.

*Ame.* The Rue Jombert!

*Mor.* Saw me!

*Both.* Yes, yes! Why, the deuce, man, I am not near-sighted. I saw you perfectly well—you were coming out of No. 19. I ran after you, but bah! your cab drove off so fast!

*Mor.* [*Aside.*] I wish to heaven it had smashed you, you old blab! [*Aloud.*] Why yes, I recollect now; I *was* in the Rue Jombert just about two o'clock. I went to a banker there about some discounts.

*Both.* Banker! No. 19! There isn't the ghost of a banker there!

*Ame.* What?

*Both.* I attend the whole house.

*Annie.* [*Aside.*] Poor Mr. Morris! [*Goes up* L. *of* BOTHERER.

*Both.* First floor, M. d'Haussay, the deputy; Second floor, M. Lambert, foreign office; third floor——

*Mor.* [*Angrily.*] For heaven's sake, don't make out an assessor's list of them! I went to see M. d'Haussay.

*Both.* Why, he's in the country!

*Ame.* In the country!

*Mor.* No, he isn't; he has come back!

*Both.* Pooh! pooh!

*Mor.* This very morning!

*Both.* He only went yesterday!

*Mor.* [*Aside.*] What torture! [*Aloud.*] Well, what of that? Can't one change one's mind on the way?

*Ame.* [*Ironically.*] Eh! Of course, doctor, my husband is right. You set off to-day for the country; you come back to-morrow. What more natural? and then, you know, a representative of the people may very well be a banker—it's not unconstitutional in France, I suppose, though I never heard of a banker who represented the people in America.

*Mor.* [*Aside.*] She's making fun of me! Can't blame her!

*Both.* The Baron d'Haussay a banker! Why, he's a chemist. A chemical banker!

*Mor.* [*Quickly.*] Why not? The Chemical Bank is the only bank that has not gone in New York. He's their agent; that's the reason I went to him. [*Aside.*] *Hold your tongue!*

*Both.* [*Amazed.*] Eh! what!

*Annie.* [*On the other side.*] *Hold your tongue!*

*Both.* [*Confused.*] Eh! what! What's the matter with them all?

*Ame.* [*Aside.*] He has *lied* to me!

*Annie.* [*Aside.*] Amelia will break out, and then there will be a scene!

*Enter* JOSEPH.

*Mor.* [*To* JOSEPH.] Well now! What do you want?

*Jos.* I beg pardon, sir; but Madame Botherer's maid has just come down to speak with her.

*Annie.* Ah! yes, I know what she wants. [*Aside.*] That'll make a diversion.

*Both.* What's it, my duck?

*Annie.* Oh, nothing; something about a dress. Amelia dear, will you come with me?

*Ame.* [*Agitated.*] Yes, yes; I will come with you.

*Annie.* [*To her husband.*] You'll find me up stairs.

*Ame.* [*Looking at her husband.*] Oh, I long to be alone with him!

*Mor.* [*Meeting his wife's eye.*] Oh, Lord! I am in for it now!

[*Exeunt* AMELIA *and* ANNIE, C.

*Mor.* [*To* BOTHERER.] You are charming! you are obliging—I am highly indebted to you!

*Both.* Now then! what is going on? What ails you? Have you a fever?

*Mor.* Are you blind? Are you an owl? Didn't you see what I was going through with?

*Both.* Now, now! let's be calm, let's be calm, my dear friend! One must be calm when one is undergoing a diagnosis. [*Proceeds to feel his pulse.*] Where is the pain?

*Mor.* Bah! I am just as well as you are! [BOTHERER *looks at him, amazed.*] What the devil made you tell my wife you saw me in the Rue Jombert?

*Both.* Why? was it wrong? [*Confused.*

*Mor.* [R.] Yes, by Jupiter, it *was* wrong. If I choose to say to Amelia that I passed the whole day at the exchange, I should like to know why you must set about undeceiving her?

*Both.* My dear friend, I am so little accustomed to snares and devices and secrets——

*Mor.* At least, when you seen me standing there, stnpid and struck dumb, you might have tried to mend matters, and patch up the business—but no! no! you must go on, and on, and on!

*Both.* It's true; I went on, and on, and on.

*Mor.* And, thanks to you, I shall have the cursedest row!

*Both.* [*Good-naturedly.*] No, no! because you went to a banker—a Chemical Bank-er!

*Mor.* Good heaven! you don't mean to say you believed that?

*Both.* Why, of course! You said so—I believed it!

*Mor.* I wish to the Lord you were my wife, indeed I do. *She* didn't believe one word of it.

*Both.* Eh! what! Then you hadn't been to see M. d'Haussay?

*Mor.* [*Angrily.*] Damn the man! I never so much as heard of him.

*Both.* Now! I knew it couldn't be so. Coming back so suddenly from the country! Discount and analysis arm-in-arm! Ah! it wasn't the least bit probable.

*Mor.* And now, when my wife demands an explanation—and she *will*—what am I to say?

*Both.* [*Amiably.*] Say! Why, what should you say? Just the truth.

*Mor.* Oh yes! that's very fine; but there are circumstances.

*Both.* There are *no* circumstances, you will say, after embracing her; for a kiss, you see, smooths the way; it is an emollient, is a kiss. You will say, "My own darling, I was coming from"—[*reflects*] —by the way, where was you coming from?

*Mor.* Coming from—I was coming from—I was coming from—the third floor.

*Both.* Ah! but the third floor is a woman.

*Mor.* Undoubtedly! and a very charming woman!

*Both.* Wretched man! I fear I am beginning to understand you. This trick, this falsehood, this third floor! Ah! what desperate symptoms! Are you, then, threatened with an attack of infidelity?

*Mor.* Oh, my heavens, you are stark mad.

*Both.* [*Severely.*] M. Morris, how do you explain your visits to that young and lovely woman?

*Mor.* *You* visit her yourself.

*Both.* Oh, I go as her physician.

*Mor.* I go as her broker.

*Both.* [*Surprised.*] Ah!

*Mor.* Yes, I buy American stocks for her; when you saw me there to-day, I had just been consulting with her.

*Both.* No, really? [*Takes his hand.*] My dear friend, I am *too* glad to hear what you say. I was beginning to think—but since you are her broker, it changes the whole matter. Forgive me, my dear friend forgive me.

*Mor.* Moreover, you knew I was acquainted with that lady, for I have often asked you after her.

*Both.* You are right, you are perfectly right. But my dear friend, I don't see that you shouldn't tell all that to your dear wife.

*Mor.* Now then, you don't! I put it to yourself: When a lovely invalid sends for you, do you talk about her to Mrs. Botherer.

*Both.* Yes.

*Mor.* But, if it is a woman of fashion, sick with a whim, and sitting in a delicious boudoir, and supporting her pensive head upon a dimpled hand, and burying in cushions of velvet, an exquisite arm. Do you tell all that to your wife?

*Both.* Yes, I tell my wife everything; besides exquisite arms, dimpled hands, all that is one to me. I look at everything in a scientific point of view.

*Mor.* And I look at everything in a financial point of view, but the difference is, you see, you have a confiding wife, and I a most jealous—

*Both.* That is because you hide things from her. Now look at Annie, she is still as a toad, and yet she knows that I go to see that lady in the Rue Jombert; that I go there very often—she is a most extraordinary patient—sends for me half a dozen times a day—now it is a headache, then neuralgia—but it don't signify—whatever else it is, it is always her francs for me. By the way, I just came from her.

*Mor.* [*Astonished.*] What! this evening.

*Both.* Yes, just as I was going to dinner she sent for me.

*Mor.* [*Affected indifference.*] And what was the matter to-night.

*Both.* [*Gaily.*] Oh, to-night was the turn of her headache.

*Mor.* [*Aside and vexed.*] Devil! Then she cannot receive me!

*Both.* I heard the door shut, perhaps my wife—[*Looking out.*] No; it is my dear Annie going up stairs. I'll go after her. Dear soul, she can't live without me. Ah Morris, Morris, follow my example, give up your stratagems, your deceits. See, there you tremble like an aspen to the thought of your wife, while I march to meet mine, my heart at rest, my head up like another Bayard. Good-bye. [*Exit*, C.

*Mor.* Ah, can't receive me! Confounded headache, and yet when I left at the Cafè Vessau, she said this evening. How annoying it is! and yet I can't help laughing when I think of that poor Doctor Botherer unconsciously playing the part of Cupid's post-man. Headache —can't be seen—neuralgia—I am expected; and he never suspects anything. [*Changes tone.*] What do I gain by it? In the street I am afraid somebody will see me. At home I am afraid that I shall betray myself. I am afraid to drink a glass of champagne in mine own house, and now that muddle-headed Botherer must come in, and stir up my wife. Heavens! here she is; the storm is about to break. Furl sails! and let the tempest pass over! now look out for thunder.

[*Sits on sofa*, L.

*Ame.* [*Coming up very gently.*] Arthur? [*He looks surprised.*] Give me your hand and forgive me!

*Mor.* What? Forgive you! *I* forgive you?

*Ame.* Just now before our friends I vexed you with tears. I vexed you—— [MORRIS *makes a sign.*] Oh! I understand you—men do not like to render an account of their doings, and the husband who is suspected, is already almost lost!

*Mor.* [*Rising.*] Can you believe!

*Ame.* Dearest, henceforth I shall wait for your confidence. I shall not command it.

*Mor.* [*Aside.*] No more questions. No more quarrels! What a splendid operation.

*Ame.* Now, you are not still angry with me?

*Mor.* I! Can you imagine it?

*Ame.* [*Taking up his hat from the piano.*] Now that peace is made, I will not detain you.

*Mor.* What!

*Ame.* Did you not say that you had an engagement. My dear I ask nothing about it. Go and come home—well—as soon as you can.

*Morris.* [*Aside.*] Since I have no reasons for going out, suppose I make a virtue of staying at home.

*Ame.* You do not go?

*Mor.* No, my darling, and I *shall* not go!

*Ame.* What! not go? And this business?

*Mor.* Oh, my dear, there is no business pressing? You are so good, so sweet, I must have the pleasure of passing the evening with you.

*Ame.* Truly? And you will make such a sacrifice?

*Mor.* Sacrifice! not a bit of it!

*Ame.* I am so afraid you will find it tedious.

*Mor.* Tedious! with you! with my own dear wife!

*Ame.* Ah, how happy you make me. [*Aside.*] How lucky I took Annie's advice. [*Aloud.*] Arthur?

[MORRIS *embraces his wife, just on the moment when* LAMOURET *enters,* C. *comes down,* R.

*Lam.* [*Astonished.*] Oh! [*Aside.*] Pretty business this! I've stumbled on a making up.

*Mor.* Ah! Lamouret, it's you, is it?

*Ame.* Oh, yes, I had forgotten to tell you that Mr. Lamouret was here once before this evening.

*Mor.* Indeed!

*Lam.* Yes, I stopped as I was going by.

*Mor.* But what is the matter with you? You look troubled.

*Ame.* Perhaps the business that took you out, awhile ago.

*Lam.* Precisely.

*Ame.* Nothing gone wrong, I hope?

*Lam.* Everything, Madame! I have thrown away a cab fare, and an hour's time. I've lost a chance.

*Mor.* Oh, well, you'll find another one of these days, I dare say.

*Lam.* So I hope. [*Aside.*] Where, in the devil's name, *did* he dine?

*Ame.* [*Aside.*] Now I wonder if he is going to stay.

*Lam.* So, Morris, you mean to stay at home, do you?

*Mor.* Yes, my dear fellow, I consecrate this hour to my wife.

*Lam.* [*Forcing a smile.*] Charming! [*Aside.*] And I expected to find them at sixes and sevens!

*Mor.* [*Going up.*] I'll just send for Botherer and his wife. We'll have some whist. Joseph?

*Lam.* And if I don't intrude.

*Mor.* Nonsense! I thought you always went to the club, like all the rest of the lazy men.

*Lam.* Not till midnight. I meet some friends there—the Viscount Mangerin, Colonel de Sabres.

*Mor.* Ah! Colonel de Sabres. I know him, he dabbles in stocks.

*Lam.* And he dabbles in love too. [*Aside.*] He's in love now with a charming widow, they say, Madame Florentine.

*Mor.* [*Quickly.*] You know her?

*Lam.* Not at all! [*Aside.*] I only know that she lives in the Rue Jombert.

*Mor.* [*Coughing furiously.*] Joseph?

*Enter* JOSEPH, C.

Joseph, go for some ice creams.

*Ame.* What?

*Mor.* Ice creams, my dear. You know you always like them, and though you can't be persuaded that Tortoni's is as good as Maillard's——

*Ame.* It is very kind of you!

*Lam.* By Jove! playing the honeymoon!

*Mor.* And Joseph! go to the doctor's, and beg him and his wife to come and take a hand with us after supper. [*Exit*, JOSEPH, C.

*Lam.* Oh, don't send Joseph. I'll take the message myself. I'm going to consult the Doctor about my palpitations. [*Lays his hand on his heart.*] This organ is so sensitive!

*Mor.* Pooh! stuff! nonsense! You are only hypochondriac—get married.

*Lam.* [*Going out.*] I'll be back directly. [*Aside.*] Let's see what I can do in the Rue Jombert. Nothing going on here! [*Exit*, C.

*Ame.* And now, dear Arthur, while we wait for our friends, come and sit by my side. [*She draws an arm-chair to the fire.*

*Mor.* Just so; let's sit down.

*Ame.* Ah, my dear Arthur, how long it is since I have had you so to myself.

*Mor.* [*Holding out his hand.*] There is a good time coming, my dear, you know, and what is so good as to be stretched out comfortably in a good arm chair?

*Ame.* [*Taking the chair at his side.*] And near one's wife.

*Mor.* And near the fire.

*Ame.* One has so many things to say.

*Mor.* [*Tenderly.*] So many things, dearest child. [*Changes his tone.*] Don't you think the chimney smokes?

*Ame.* Not at all!

*Mor.* Perhaps not, perhaps it's only a notion.

*Ame.* [*Tenderly.*] Arthur!

*Mor.* [*Taking up the newspaper.*] Just allow me, darling, to glance at the article about these French Chambers.

*Ame.* Oh, what are you going to bury yourself in!

*Mor.* Nothing! nothing, only I didn't see the papers to-day, and it's so interesting. I can't get over my New York habits. [*Tenderly.*] You wouldn't have me get over my New York habits.

*Ame.* [*Tenderly.*] No, dearest, not I.

*Mor.* But this is so odd. A "Poll tax on dogs," "Belgian coals"—

*Ame.* Now, darling, pray put it down. I don't know anything about your politics.

*Mor.* Ah, they have killed the tax. That's all I cared to know. [*Throws the paper down.*

*Ame.* [*Joyously.*] Now let us speak of ourselves—of our memories—of——

*Mor.* Of our love.

*Ame.* I hardly dared pronounce that word.

*Mor.* Why so?

*Ame.* Why, I sometimes have thought you love me less than when—

*Mor.* Love you less! I that am always, as much as possible, that is, at your side. I that at this moment—— Confound it the chimney certainly *does* smoke!

*Ame.* [*Vexed.*] Still the chimney!

*Mor.* They can't build a chimney in France. I've sent to the landlord at last.

*Ame.* Shall I open the window?

*Mor.* Oh, no, thank you. Not to freeze us—does your chimney smoke?

*Ame.* [*Crossly.*] Not a bit.

*Mor.* So much for taking a house. You preferred it, you know, dear, and here we are caught. Confounded smoke—and we were talking so nicely. What were we talking about?

*Ame.* Oh, I've forgotten. Ah, shall I play for you a little?

*Mor.* [*Stretching out in his chair.*] Yes, yes, that is just the thing. Sing, dear, sing, and I will be your audience. I'll applaud you like a whole academy gallery.

*Ame.* And I've just learned a new romance, "Thy heart to me is closed."

*Mor.* Oh, fie! don't say that! I prefer something gay and brilliant. [*Aside.*] It keeps me awake.

*Ame.* Ah! here's one—"We're all Noddin'."

*Mor.* We're all noddin'. I shall imagine I'm in an auction room.

*Ame.* I'll see what else I have. [*Turns over her music.* MORRIS *meanwhile falls asleep in his chair.*] Ah, here is something gay, Arthur! Arthur!

*Mor.* [*Dreaming.*] Coachman! driver! to the opera house.

*Ame.* [*Coming up amazed.*] What does he say?

*Mor.* To the opera ball!

*Ame.* Ah, he is asleep. He loves me no more.

[*She dashes away a tear, at the same moment the door opens.*

*Lam.* [*Outside.*] Come in, my dear madam, come in, you are expected.

*Ame.* [*Seizing her husband by the arm.*] Arthur, somebody is coming!

*Mor.* [*Jumping up.*] "We won't go home till morning." [*Aside.*] I believe I was asleep.

*Enter* ANNIE *with* LAMOURET.

*Annie.* Ah! what a charming idea—an improvised *soiree.* It was your thought, was it not, Monsieur Morris? Allow me to congratulate you on its success!

[MORRIS *goes down and prepares the whist table.*

*Both.* [*Outside.*] My wife? Where is my wife?

*Annie.* Now hear him. I can't once amuse myself without him.

*Enter* BOTHERER, *a letter in his hand.*

*Both.* Here I am! here I am! Whist! Ice creams! ah, ha! Count us with you. Me and my wife!

*Annie.* Of course.

*Both.* My own darling, I am perfectly wretched. A dreadful press of business—it will make you miserable. I must quit you at midnight!

*Annie.* Indeed! And why?

*Both.* [*With the letter.*] My colleague, Desgranges, is ill. I must go to the hospital in his place.

*Annie.* Oh, what can one say? Duty is duty. [*Aside.*] I knew all about it three hours ago.

*Both.* But you are so unhappy whenever I leave you.

*Lam.* [*Aside.*] I've tumbled into a dove cot, by Jove!

*Both.* [*Aside to* MORRIS.] I say, my friend, the broker, I've just come from the Rue Jombert!

*Mor.* What! Now?

*Both.* Yes, found a note from her up stairs. "Come, come—I am dying—quick!" I hurry off.

*Mor.* Well?

*Both.* [*Gaily.*] Headache gone! the neuralgia come on.

*Mor.* Indeed! neuralgia?

*Both.* Ordered some barley-water with sugar in it, and charged ten francs!

*Mor.* [*Aside.*] Neuralgia! she expects me, and I've promised to stay here!

*Ame.* [*From the whist table.*] Dear, are you coming to make the fourth with Dr. and Mrs. Botherer.

*Mor.* Oh, certainly! [*Aside.*] Devil take it, it might have been done on purpose. It's infernal! [*Crosses,* L.

*Enter* JOSEPH.

Ah! Joseph, how about that ice cream?

*Jos.* I can't get any, sir, there are so many ordered out.

*Mor.* [*Aside.*] What an idea.

*Jos.* I went too late, sir.

*Mor.* Nonsense! it's only your ignorance; any Yankee would find enough in five minutes!

*Ame.* Oh, well, its a trifle.

*Annie.* We'll get along very well without them.

*Jos.* And, indeed, sir, they can't be got.

*Mor.* [*Rising.*] Pooh! I'll bet I'll find them.

*Ame.* What, my dear, you don't think of going out yourself, surely?

*Both.* And so cold as it is?

*Mor.* Only a quarter of an hour, not a moment longer. Lamouret pray take my hand. [*They all look up and remonstrate.*] Nonsense, back in five minutes, with a whole Arctic region of ice creams!

[*Goes out. They take up the cards.*

*Both.* [*Rises and goes to window,* L.] I don't believe he'll be able to find the Rue Glacier. I'll see which way he goes. There—I knew it—there he goes toward the Rue Jombert.

*Ame.* The Rue Jombert! Ah! [*Faints in chair.*

*Both.* She faints! The *sal volatile!* Quick!

[LAMOURET *hands a surgeon's* [illegible] *in mistake.*

END OF ACT I

## ACT II.

SCENE I.—*Saloon at the Maison d'Or—Richly furnished.*

COLONEL DE SABRES, R., DE LUCENAY, L., MANGERIN, LAMOURET, R., *Grouped around a small table, and drinking punch.*

*Col.* Now that you've tossed off your punch, my dear Monsieur Lamouret, pray toss us off your story.

*Lam.* Really? won't it bore you?

*Col.* Quite the contrary. You amuse us extremely.

[LAMOURET *bows and drinks.*

*Luce.* By all means. We are comfortable here. The ball will keep, and as a husband I like to know what is going on.

*Col.* [*Putting down his glass.*] You were saying the husband went out for some ice creams.

*Lam.* Leaving me his substitute at the whist table.

*Col.* Well?

*Luce.* Then?

*Lam.* Half an hour—an hour went by, Marlborough did not come back——

*All.* Marlborough!

*Lam.* The husband! I hide the real name, you know.

*Col.* Ah, you are very discreet, for a gossip—pray go on.

*Lam.* You will understand, gentlemen, that this prolonged absence began to seem suspicious. Every body was embarrassed—every body played badly—the lady of the house looked miserably at the clock, and I—I laughed in my sleeve, thinking, "bravo! this is very fine! this is warming up."

*Luce.* But at last? for, after all, a husband *must* sooner or later come home!

*Lam.* When we broke up at midnight he hadn't reappeared!

*All.* Really?

*Lam.* Still absent under a pretext of buying ice cream.

*Col.* Did he go to Norway after them?

*Lam.* So you see it's quite clear that here we have a husband breaking bounds.

*Luce.* And breaking forever I should say!

*Lam.* Well, these are the facts. As for the fruit of them—

[*He trims his moustaches.*

*Luce.* [*Rising and passing to the left of* LAMOURET.] What a dangerous fellow you are! We must look out for you?

*Lam.* Let the story be a warning to you, my dear de Lucenay, who have a charming wife, and pass all your nights at the club—at the balls.

*Luce.* [*Sitting down again.*] Oh! my wife adores me!

*Lam.* No doubt, but she is an ardent, passionate creature who wouldn't easily put up with an affront. [*Aside.*] And I am always ready to avenge injured innocence!

*Col.* [*Solemly.*] My dear Monsieur Lamouret, do you know that if I were the husband of whom you have been talking to us, and should get wind of your gracious projects, I should give you just so long to live, as it would take to go from your rooms to the Bois de Vincennes. Say, with a good carriage—mine for instance—just twenty-five minutes!

*Lam.* By Jove! Colonel, you don't mean it.

*Col.* [*Taking out a cigar.*] I fall in love with a woman, and I fall out again, but I won't have any man pull me out. For instance last week I was paying court to a lady. There was a young coxcomb who undertook to cut me out. I surprised him one morning. Came in on the two.

*Lam.* And there was a dreadful quarrel?

*Col.* Not at all! just these words: I said, "Sir, my carriage is at your orders." Half an hour afterwards we were facing each other at fifteen paces. He paid no more visits. [*Hands* LAMOURET *his cigars.*] Do you smoke?

*Lam.* No, thank you, don't use them. [*Aside.*] If I got into a row with that fellow, I should inform the police.

*Luce.* Well, do we sup here together? [*Crosses to* R., *table.*

*Man.* With all my heart!

*Luce.* And you Colonel?

*Col.* Oh, certainly! I went to-night to the Rue Jombert to bring a lady to the ball, but there was a neuralgia, and I saw a scene, just for a vase of flowers that the maid wished to put out on the balcony, and her mistress ran up, took the flowers away and boxed her ears. So the maid began to cry, and the mistress to scold. One "leave my house," the other "I will be revenged," and I took my hat, and bowed myself out!

*Luce.* So you are alone at the ball?

*Lam.* Oh, look for a consolation! Show your skill in finding a conquest!

*Col.* My dear sir, pray preach by practice. You have the air of a conqueror. You talk of your prowess, and you are always alone You walk about alone, you sup alone. Is it a vow you have taken?

*Lam.* [*Disdainfully.*] I scorn facile victories!

*Col.* [*Coming towards him.*] Eh! we didn't make a mistake. There is no victory facile to a man who has not one, at least, of three good qualities. One must be either handsome, rich, or witty, and on these scores, my dear sir——

*Lam.* Eh! I don't quite see?

*Luce.* Handsome!

*Col.* Rich!——

*Luce.* Or witty.

*Lam.* [*Vexed.*] Ah, laugh away, gentlemen. I'll make a bet with you.

*Col.* Good! What is it?

*Lam.* Let's bet supper that before an hour's time, I shall have made a conquest. [*All laughing violently.*

*Col.* I take the bet, however. [BAPTISTE *comes in with another waiter.*] I say, waiter, keep a cabinet for three o'clock, and put some champagne on the ice. And now, gentlemen, to the opera ball.

[*Music strikes up a waltz.* MORRIS *comes in as the* COLONEL *and* LAMOURET *go out, talking together,* 2 D. E. MORRIS *seeing* LAMOURET, *wheels about and buries his face in a newspaper, which he finds on the chimney-piece.*

*Mor.* [*Coming down forward.*] Confound that Lamouret! What's he doing here? And that was the Colonel with him, I'm sure; and I think I saw Lucenay, the broker. Well, its all right now, and they are gone; but I've met every body I know in Paris, to-night, at the Ball, and half of New York besides, it seems to me! Waiter?

*Bap.* [R.] Sir?

*Mor.* [L. *To himself.*] In the boxes, in the corridor, every where, somebody in the way. "Ah! how d'ye do?" and "how's your wife?" I suppose because one's married, one mayn't go to a masked ball. Waiter?

*Bap.* Sir?

*Mor.* I kept bobbing my head about till I thought it would drop off. I flattened my nose for ten minutes against a pillar. Waiter? [*Angrily.*

*Bap.* Sir!

*Mor.* A private room and supper for two.

*Bap.* Oh, you needn't say that, sir?

*Mor.* What!

*Bap.* Gentlemen don't come here alone, sir. No dances here, sir.

*Mor.* Very well, I don't want any of your observations. [*Lower.*] Have you a cabinet with a private entrance on the small stairway?

*Bap.* We have two, sir, No. 10, and No. 8. The famous No. 8.

*Mor.* Famous or infamous, I take No. 8.

*Bap.* Very good, sir.

*Mor.* At three o'clock when I come in by *that* door, a lady will come in by *that* door!

*Bap.* On the little stairway? All right, sir.

*Mor.* You will let her in?

*Bap.* [*Mysteriously.*] Sir? [*Aside.*] That's a married man. [*Music ceases.*

*Mor.* Give me the bill of fare and a glass of absinth.

*Bap.* Immediately sir! Don't they keep up their lark, though, these married men. When I save some money, I'll marry too, and have some fun. [*Exit,* C.

*Mor.* Well, what next, I wonder. Here have I begun the night by standing sentry for 2 hours in the balcony of the 3d floor, Rue Jombert, while Colonel de Sabres sat inside, with his feet at the fire making love to Madame Florentine. I was all of a shiver in the fog without, he all of a glow in the cozy room. [*Rubs his shoulders.*] That's the way people take rheumatisms, and then they go home, and say, "there was a window open behind me in the omnibus coming home," or I got my feet wet out shooting. And then there was that devilish servant girl came near opening the window with the pot of flowers.

I try to be gay. I am indefatigable in hunting up amusement, it's of no use! I can't shake off a swarm of thoughts! What does it all come to? What shall I say to my wife to-morrow? Oh, Lord, if we could only have a revolution! or a great fire! or an earthquake! but no, it's not my luck!

*Bap.* [*Comes back.*] Here sir, is the bill of fare and the absinth. And if Monsieur will pass into the famous No. 8, he will find pens and ink to order his own supper with.

[*Goes into the* R. H. *cabinet,* 2 E. R., *and leaves the door open.*

*Mor.* After all what does it signify, let me go home late or early, I'm sure to be scolded! Well! Waiter, I say?

[*Goes into the cabinet.*

[*At the same moment a woman in a black domino, masked, comes in at the middle door,* L. U. D. AMELIA *and* BOTHERER—*he wearing green spectacles, and with his collar turned up to hide the lower part of his face.*

*Ame.* [*Taking off her mask.*] Come, doctor, come! I saw him come in here!

*Both.* [*Taking off the glasses.*] Are you quite sure? Quite?

*Ame.* Very sure? It was he whom we saw under the peristile of the Opera House, just when I was giving up the search and asking you to take me home.

*Both.* Much, be it observed, to my satisfaction and pleasure!

*Ame.* And I am sure I saw him come over here.

*Both.* And so, shall we go home?

*Ame.* Oh! doctor, not yet! not yet!

*Both.* Now, my dear lady, allow me! you——

*Ame.* Monsieur Morris is here, certainly, but is he here alone, is he waiting here for some one. Ah, doctor, the peace of my whole life is at stake!

*Both.* Yes, madam, but what is becoming of *my* peace—*my* repose. [*Takes out his watch.*] It is two o'clock, madam, and ever since midnight I have been enjoying the honor of following about with you after your husband, by the sacrifice of my duties as a husband and as a physician!

*Ame.* Ah! yes, reproach me with this service.

*Both.* Far from it! but——

*Ame.* To whom else could I apply?

*Both.* I am much flattered by your choice, but——

*Ame.* But at midnight, when Arthur still stayed away, my tears could no longer be restrained, then indignation came to my aid. I remembered what my husband had said in his sleep.

*Both.* Eh? is he a somnambulist?

*Ame.* At once my resolution was taken. I thought of the Opera, put on this black domino—to go alone was impossible—I heard a door shut, heard you come down stairs——

*Both.* I had just given my farewell kiss to Annie, and whilst that dear soul was putting up her curls, I set off for my hospital——

*Ame.* At once I thought of you—of your kindness—I resolved to appeal to you——

*Both.* You took my arm, Madam, you captured me. I had fallen into an ambush. It was useless to resist.

*Ame.* Ah! if you knew what jealousy is!

*Both.* Jealousy? Not know what it is! It's an acute disease, Madame, but there's nothing in the Materia Medica to reach it, and not much art——

*Ame.* Hush! he *isn't* alone!

*Both.* [*Aside.*] I shall never get away! [*Goes toward cabinet,* R.

*Ame.* Somebody's talking with him.

*Both.* [*Listening.*] It's a male voice!

*Ame.* Do you think so?

*Both.* [*Decidedly.*] No female lungs there, Madame. The waiter, I take it, he is not a Ganymede, nor your husband a Jupiter, so I suppose you won't be jealous of the waiter.

*Ame.* Oh these emotions are unendurable!

*Both.* Then, dear lady, don't endure them. Pray come away. The thing is clear, Mr. Morris would come to the ball, and without you. He will sup and without you, and it's atrocious I admit. No husband has a right to sup without his wife; but he might have done worse. So do let's come away. Eh?

*Ame.* Just one moment, doctor, to see his friends arrive!

*Both.* [*Aside.*] Oh, Lord! Oh, Lord! Now she must wait for the friends! [*Looks at his watch.*] A quarter past two. [*Aloud.*] But, madam, if your husband should pass out and find himself dogged—find *me* at his heels.

*Ame.* Oh, he'll never know it, he shan't know it, and thanks to this mask——

*Both.* But *I've* no mask!

*Ame.* Oh, with those goggles, and that coat collar.

*Both.* Decidedly, madam, you are too unreasonable! I shall go, I am a physician, madam. Think of my patients, madam, if one should die. I am a husband, I owe it to my wife.

*Ame.* Somebody's coming—hold your tongue.

[*Puts on her mask.* BOTHERER *his glasses, and they converse together.*

*Enter* MORRIS *followed by* BAPTISTE, R. D.

*Mor.* Now you understand, *at three o'clock.* Oh! somebody here! [*He turns up his coat collar.*

*Bap.* [*Whispering* MORRIS.] All right, sir.

*Mor.* It seems to me I know every body I meet, and meet every body I know. [*Goes up and then slyly walks around* BOTHERER *and* AMELIA.] Ah! it would appear that gentleman too is not over anxious to be recognised. Another noodle like unto myself!

*Both.* [*To* AMELIA.] He's going!

*Ame.* Let's follow him.

*Both.* [*Raising his voice.*] Ah! no, indeed!

*Ame.* Speak low!

*Mor.* [*Stopping.*] Eh? Don't I know that voice?

[*He looks at* BOTHERER *and* BOTHERER *looks at him, their eyes meet.*

*Both.* [*To* AMELIA.] He's watching us!

*Mor.* [*Coming down.*] The deuce! its very odd—that figure—that overcoat, by Jove it's he! [*Aloud.*] I say, Botherer!

*Both.* [*Involuntary.*] Eh!

*Mor.* Ah! ha: my boy. I've caught you, have I?

*Both.* [*Aside.*] I'm caught!

*Ame.* [*Aside.*] I *shall* be!

*Mor.* Ho! ho! my medical St. Anthony. this is the way we go to an hospital, is it? Are you studying the "*Maris à Dorée*," from the scientific point of view? Ha! ha!

*Both.* [*Earnestly.*] I assure you——

*Mor.* [*Roaring with laughter.*] Ah, imposter! imposter! Now, don't say a word! and to think how you took me in, and, as we say in New York, "did for me," and I thought you so green! oh! oh oh!

*Both.* But I do declare to you——

*Ame.* [*To* BOTHERER.] In the name of heaven, not one word.

*Mor.* Unhappy Botherer, if only your wife knew?

*Both.* My wife! [AMELIA *stops him.*

*Mor.* Oh! good gracious I didn't mean to say it. My dear doctor I am as bad as you were about the Rue Jombert. [AMELIA *starts.*] Just as bad. I beg a thousand pardons! And you, my dear madam, must excuse me, I can only say that, like a poor friend here, I too have a wife!

*Both.* Now he's in for it!

*Mor.* [*With an afflicted air.*] Alas! yes, my dear madam, we are married. Don't blame us—we are very sorry for it.

*Both.* Morris! [AMELIA *stops him.*

*Mor.* [*To* BOTHERER.] Be quiet! [*To himself.*] I'll set it all right! Ah, madam, if you knew the misery, the monotony of married life

*Both.* [*Aside.*] Go a head then! as you say in New York.

*Mor.* You shouldn't reprove us for the brief moments we give to the domestic Bastille.

*Both.* [*Aside.*] Blockhead! blockhead!

*Mor.* For as soon as we can break bounds, you wouldn't think us the same men. We are all life and animation. My friend, the doctor, here at home a very Cato, a very saint for purity, once get him off on such an expedition as this, and he becomes more amusing than a light comedian, throws up his heels like a rope dancer.

*Both.* Confound his impudence!

*Mor.* He kicks off his respectability like a pair of boots. [AMELIA *can hardly restrain the indignation of* BOTHERER.] But I see I make three, so heaven forbid I should stay. I expect to be as well as yourself, my gay Esculapius, at three o'clock. [*Bows to* MADAME.

*Ame.* [*Aside.*] Heavens!

*Mor.* Couldn't we all sup together, and make a night of it?

*Ame.* [*On* BOTHERER'S *arm.*] Ah!

*Both.* [*To* MORRIS.] Hold your tongue, sir! If you knew before whom you were speaking——

*Mor.* Oh! no offence; I can respect the incognito of beauty. [*Bows in a conceited manner.*] Madame, adieu! [*To* BOTHERER.] Adieu, you young rascal! [*Exit, laughing immoderately*, L. U. E.

*Ame.* Oh, doctor! A chair! a chair!

*Both.* [*Catching her as she is about to faint.*] Now then! now then!

*Ame.* Air, air! I am fainting!

*Both.* [*Seating her.*] Well now, the job's perfect! [*Rings the bell.* Waiter! Waiter!

*Enter* BAPTISTE. C.

*Bap.* Madame? [*Down* L.

*Both.* Quick! a private room a cabinet!

[*Hands the sal volatile out of his medical bag to* AMELIA.

*Bap.* Ah! the lady is unwell!

*Both.* What is that to you? Be in a hurry. [*To* AMELIA.] Courage! Courage!

*Amelia.* [*Rising.*] Oh, It'll be soon over!

*Both.* Heaven grant it. My poor head is going.

*Bap.* The room is ready, sir.

*Ame.* [*As they go to it.*] Oh! why did I ever come here.

[*Exit,* L. D. 2 E.

*Both.* [*Exasperated.*] Exactly! why did I ever come here! [*Looks at the clock.*] 20 minutes to 3.

*Bap.* What shall I order, sir.

*Both.* An infusion of Valerian, and be quick! [*Goes in* L.

*Bap.* An infusion of Valerian! why it's a dose! fancy me roaring down stairs, "Infusion of Valerian for one!" [*As* BAPTISTE *speaks* ANNIE *comes in, in a blue dominie, looking about her.*] *Apart.*] Ah, a lovely domino. [*Aloud.*] Madame is looking for some one?

*Annie.* Yes, three ladies.

*Bap.* Three ladies?

*Annie.* You have not seen them?

*Bap.* Three ladies dressed as firemen, in company with eight gen tlemen?

*Annie.* [*Frightened.*] Good heavens, no! three ladies alone!

*Bap.* Alone? we haven't any such here, Madame! but it's still early, Madame.

*Annie.* I suppose I may wait?

*Bap.* Certainly, and what shall I bring Madame? A Punch?

*Annie.* [*Aside.*] I must take something. [*Aloud.*] A Punch? No indeed! a glass of sugar and water.

*Bap.* Infusion of Valerian! sugar and water!

*Voice outside.* Waiter, waiter! 3 champagne punches.

*Bap.* [*Going out* C.] Ah! there is the genuine article!

*Annie.* [*Taking off her mask.*] What a woman, to leave me alone in that mob. Ah! Madame Giraud I shan't forget this trick! But what has become of them? I can't go home alone; I dont wan't the servants to know of the matter. And there's my poor husband who thinks me sound asleep. [*The door opens.*] Heaven's, somebody's coming. [*Puts on her mask again.*

*Both.* [*Coming out and speahing to Amelio within.*] I'll fetch a cab! Eh! what do you say. [*Goes back for a moment.*

*Annie.* Why it's himself! It's Botherer! It's a dream! but no, I'm wide awake *as usual.* [*Laughs.*] Ah, Botherer that's your way of watching the sick, is it? drinking here with your colleagues, wetting your grave old whiskers with champagne, it's very odd, very lucky too—I'll just fool him a little, and then we'll go home together, or back to the ball which was so funny.

*Both.* [*Re-enters.—To himself.*] She's come to her senses, she agrees to go home. [*Annie takes his arm as he is going out.*] I beg your pardon Madame, you've made a slight mistake.

*Annie.* [*Disguising her voice.*] Oh, no!

*Both.* No? But you have though! Do you know me?

*Annie.* Ah, yes!

*Both.* [*Aside.*] Humph! well it's some patient of mine. [*Aloud.*] I am quite sure Madame, I am can't be of any use to you just now.

*Annie.* Oh, yes, you can.

*Both.* Are you ill? Then go home at once, and send for me. I don't prescribe here, and I beg you to let go my arm. If anybody should see us in this position, it would compromise me as a married man.

*Annie.* [*Following him.*] Good Botherer, always thinking of me.

*Both.* [*Trying to go.*] Madame! *au revoir*!

*Annie.* [*Stopping him.*] Allow me!

*Both.* [*Aside.*] Some designing wretch. [*Aloud.*] Madame, I am in haste. May I ask what you want?

*Annie.* A service.

*Both.* [*Aside.*] Another woman! [*Aloud.*] Madame, do you happen to have a husband.

*Annie.* Yes.

*Both.* Then I'll bet he's caracoling about at the ball.

*Annie.* Yes, alas!

*Both.* Are you running after him?

*Annie.* Exactly.

*Both.* And you want me to travel in your caleche?

*Annie.* You've hit it.

*Both.* [*Aside.*] Upon my honor the best thing I can do, is to laugh at it all. [*Aloud.*] My angel, you must let me go, I have wasted enough time, though I am going for a cab. Release me, if you please. Good Lord, Madame, I say you you are pinching me.

*Annie,* [*Choking with laughter.*] Monsieur, I intreat you.

*Both.* [*Aside.*] It's an adventuress. Let's destroy her hopes. [*Aloud.*] Madame. I am here with a friend.

*Annie.* [*Gaily.*] Ah!

*Both.* With a lovely friend, Madame.

*Annie.* [*Troubled.*] Eh?

*Both.* A lovely woman, Madame.

*Annie.* A woman.

*Both.* Moreover, she is as jealous, and as savage as a tigress!

*Annie.* [*Aside.*] Oh, heavens!

*Both.* And I'm going for a cab to take her away, sorry to be obliged to quit you so abruptly.

*Annie.* [*Staggering to a chair.*] Oh, I shall faint.

*Both.* [*Aside.*] Oh, I know all about that sort of thing! now I'm rid of her! this night ought to balance two nights on duty in the National Guard. [*Exit,* L. U. E. *Music.*

*Annie.* [*Drops her mask and falls into the chair* R.] A woman! I shall faint. [*Energetically.*] No, I won't! No! [*Rushes to door of cabinet* L. *and throws it wide open.*] Come out Madame, Come out, I say! I know all! [AMELIA *comes out.*] Heavens! Amelia!

*Ame.* Annie.

*Annie.* You with my husband.

*Ame*, Oh, don't be concerned, I carried him off by force, almost, to hunt up my husband for me. My husband who is a deceiver and traitor.

*Annie*. *Your* husband. Oh, my dear, I am so delighted to hear it.

*Ame*. What!

*Annie*. Oh, excuse me, I am so glad it wasn't my husband, who is a—

*Ame*. *You* glad of that. You, who this very evening complained to me of Botherer's devotion. Why I thought you wanted him to run away from you.

*Annie*. Oh, yes, it's all very well to say that, when one's sure that he *won't* run away. But my dear, my dear. [*Takes her hand.*] What have you learned? what have you learned?

*Ame*. My husband is at the ball with a woman who is coming here to sup with him. [*Stop music.*

*Annie*. Horrible! Oh you must make a scandal—we have our rights—we must maintain them—never again shall my husband leave me *for one single minute.*

*Ame*. But you? Are you right in being here?

*Annie*. Oh, that's Madame Giraud's fault.

*Ame*. So I guessed.

*Annie*. You know what I said to you. Well, she came after Botherer had gone; she insisted, so I came, came with her friends Mesdames Fairwell and De Lucenay, and I lost them and lost her. Only I left! I, perfectly alone in the midst of a sea of promenaders, and they are so impertinent at the masked ball, you've no idea. Even Mr. Loveit was there, and would insist upon my supping with him.

*Ame*. Did he recognise you?

*Annie*. Thank fortune, no; he is such a scandal monger! At last I got away here, when I hoped to find my party, and where I did *not* expect to find you. Now tell me how *shall* I get home?

*Ame*. I can save you!

*Annie*. How?

*Ame*. You really want to get away?

*Annie*. Indeed I do!

*Ame*. And I really want to stay.

*Annie*. Well.

*Ame*. Your husband will be back in five minutes with a cab. Let us change dominos. You keep on your mask, and be miserable, cry if you can, all the way home, there the Doctor will leave you, and hurry on to his hospital.

*Annie*. Oh, that's delightful.

*Ame*. Come be quick, some one's coming. [*They go into cabinet.*

*Enter* LAMOURET *and* COL. DE SABRES, L. U E. LAMOURET *sees* ANNIE *as she retires.*

*Lam*. My blue domino. [*He runs after her but she slams the door.*

*Col*. Well my dear Monsieur Lamouret in ten minutes you'll have lost your bet.

*Lam*. In ten minutes I shall have won it!

*Luce*. Pooh, pooh! where is your conquest?

*Lam.* Wherė ? No matter, wait a little, heavenly arms, blue domino.

*Luce.* [*Laughtng.*] Heavenly blue?

*Col.* I did see you talking to something of the sort, but where is she now?

*Lam.* [*Goes* L.] There! in that cabinet. Gentlemen stand aside and don't interrupt, see, she is coming out.

[AMELIA *comes out with the mask and domino of* ANNIE.

*Ame.* [*Fancying herself alone.*] I heard a noise perhaps it was Arthur.

*Luce.* [*Aside.*] That domino is devilish like my wife.

*Ame.* [*Aside.*] Could it have been Arthur. [*Seeing* LAMOURET—*aloud.*] Oh. heavens!

*Lam.* So I've caught you at last, have I, angel! witch! siren! demon! sylph.

*Ame.* [*Aside, in fear.*] What will become of me!

*Lam.* The chase has been long, my dearest charmer but what a prize at last.

*Luce.* [*To himself.*] Just my wife's height and figure. If I wasn't sure that my wife adores me!

*Ame.* [*Aside, while* LAMOURET *makes signs to his friends.*] I shall be lost if he learns that I am here alone.

*Lam.* [*Interrupting her.*] My beauty! to the point at once. Let us take some supper.

*Ame.* [*Terrified.*] Sir!

*Lam.* You know my sentiments already. Now try my supper. I have made a declaration to you at the ball; I now offer you a bill of fare, to supper.

*Ame.* Leave me, sir. Leave me. [*She tries to go.* LAMOURET *detains her. His friends all laugh.*] Let me go, sir! [*At this moment* MORRIS *appears. She runs and takes his arm.* MORRIS *looks surprised.*]

*Mor.* Well now, what's the row?

*Lam.* [*Aside.*] Morris! My American paragon! What a discovery!

*Morris.* [*Aside.*] Lamouret! Lamouret again.

*Lam.* [*Aside.*] It was a preconcerted thing. I've got the clue to it though!

*Mor.* Madame I beg—

*Ame.* [*In a low voice and holding his arm.*] Arthur, save me.

*Morris.* [*Aside.*] Arthur, she knows me—it is Madame Florentine!

*Col.* [*Coming forward.*] I think I see Mr. Morris.

*Mor.* [*Aside and troubled.*] Colonel De Sabres!

*Col.* Ah, Ah Mr. Morris. So you have given into our Paris customs at last, have you?

*Mor.* [*Aside.*] How shall I get out of this business?

*Lam.* [*Whispers to* COLONEL.] It's the husband who went after the ice creams.

*Col.* [*Whispers.*] Ah, bah! then no wonder he's confused.

*Lam.* [*Crossing over to* LUCENAY *and* MANGERIN.] It's the ice cream man.

*Luce.* [*To himself.*] I was a fool. The idea of suspecting my wife.

*Col.* Monsieur Morris, we beg pardon for interrupting you—boreing you perhaps.

*Mor.* Oh, no! oh, no! Don't think it. [*Aside.*] What shall I do, if he grows more riotous?

*Col.* [*Whispers to* MORRIS.] A married man doesn't always care to be be recognised. [*Passes up towards his friend.*

*Mor.* [*Aside.*] Ah, a capital idea strikes me. [*Low to* AMELIA.] Be cool, dear Florentine.

*Ame.* [*Aside.*] Dear Florentine!

*Mor.* [*Bearing Amelia* L.] This lie will serve both of us. [*Aloud.*] Well, gentlemen, I have come to the opera ball, and to amuse myself. I suppose a man may amuse himself, if he is a foreigner, with his wife!

*All.* His wife!!

*Ame.* [*Aside.*] What does he mean?

*Mor.* My wife, whom I left here for a moment to find her on my return, the object of persecution.

*Col.* Which we all disown, most decidedly!

*Lam.* [*Ironically.*] Certainly, I never suspected that Mrs. Morris. [*Whispers to* COLONEL.] It is not his wife, I know.

*Col.* [*To* LAMOURET.] I'll find out whether it is or not. [*Crosses to* MORRIS.] Monsieur Morris, since we have been so fortunate as to meet Madame and yourself, I hope you will do us the honor to sup with us us.

*Lam.* [*Aside.*] Delicious! He's caught.

*Mor.* [*Aside.*] Then all's up. [*Aloud.*] Certainly, sir, we are delighted—but the fact is—indeed—we—I have engagements—in short—

*Ame.* [*Aside.*] Oh, yes. I know your engagements.

*Col.* [*Bows to* AMELIA.] Perhaps Madame will lend a kinder ear to us.

*Ame.* [*Rising.*] Yes, sir! we will sup with you, and with pleasure.

*Mor.* [*Stupified.*] Eh?

*All.* [*Thunderstruck.*] She accepts!

*Ame.* [*Aside.*] Now, I've got him, and Madame Florentine shall sup alone.

*Mor.* [*To* AMELIA.] You've ruined me!

*Lam.* [*To his friends.*] Do you see how vexed he looks.

*Luce.* In fact it's odd. I must find out—

*Bap.* [*Comes in with champagne, and whispers to* MORRIS.] The lady is in Number 8.

*Mor.* [*Amazed.*] The lady! What lady.

*Bap.* What lady! The lady you expected.

[*Points to the door and exits by another* C.

*Mor.* [*Staring at* AMELIA.] What, and who in the world then is *this* lady?

*Lam.* [*Overhearing him, and aside.*] Another! then there are *two* rivals. Another chance for me.

*Col.* Mr. Morris, you will come with us.

*Mor.* [*Embarrassed.*] Oh, yes—of course—immediately—but—exactly no—only I just wish to say one word to my wife.

*Col.* We'll wait for you.

[*The friends enter the middle door, but* LAMOURET *comes softly back.*

*Lam.* I've won my supper. [*Slips into* R. H. *cabinet.*

*Mor.* Now then, they're gone! Wéll Madame. [AMELIA *falls into a chair in a fit of laughing.*] Well, Madame, I hope you will find all this very funny. It's infamous! It's insufferable!

*Ame.* [*Disguising her voice.*] Now, why do you put yourself into such a dreadful passion?

*Mor.* Why! Why do you, Madame. Why do you accept my arm, and drag me into an awful scrape, and get me into all manner of mischief in return for my protection of you! And why do you now disguise your voice?

*Ame.* Because I don't want you to know me!

*Mor.* But Madame, *I* want to know you. I *insist* upon knowing you!

*Ame.* Who am I? Well, sir, since you insist upon knowing—I am —I am the wife of a gentleman whom you have seen on the Exchange!

*Mor.* On the Exchange?

*Ame.* And who is in this house at this moment.

*Mor.* [*Aside.*] Good heavens! it is *Lucenay!*

*Ame.* This husband of mine, whom I love, this husband is a traitor, he deceives me!

*Mor.* [*Aside.*] I always suspected that Lucenay.

*Ame.* Yes, deceives me, and for a woman, who no doubt deceives him in his turn, and for her sake, he disturbs my home and makes me wretched.

*Mor.* [*Earnestly.*] It is abominable of him!

*Ame.* And yet I dare say this woman is neither as young nor so good looking as myself.

*Mor.* [*Aside.*] I've no doubt of it, for Madame Lucenay is charming.

*Ame.* And so, sir, in my indignation, my excitement, I resolved to punish this deceiver, to punish—

*Mor.* You are quite right.

*Ame.* Yes, to revenge myself upon him. [*Rising.*] and it is of you, sir, that I ask assistance in my purpose.

*Mor.* [*Delighted.*] Of me? I, Madame! I—I renounce all other other engagements. I will be your protector—Your Champeron.

*Ame.* [*Aside and angrily.*] The base perfidious creature!

*Mor.* [*Taking up his hat.*] Whither shall I conduct Madame.

*Ame.* Anywhere! anywhere! to your own house.

*Mor.* My own house! and what will my wife say!

*They are going off, when the* COLONEL *comes out of the cabinet, a letter in his hand.*

*Col.* [*Coldly*] Allow me, sir.

*Mor.* [*Aside.*] The devil take him! [*Aloud.*] I am very sorry, but we *must* go. My wife has changed her mind.

*Col.* [*Coldly.*] Oh, I understand all about that. Be good enough to read this note, which I have just received.

*Mor.* What do I see—an anonymous letter. My name. [*Aside.*] It tells the whole story of Madame Florentine.

*Col.* It's very base I know—the pitiful revenge of some servant, who has been turned off, or of some lover who has been snubbed, but the fact remains.

*Mor.* Sir?

*Col.* Yes sir. You had an engagement here to night with Ma dame Florentine. [*Bows to* AMELIA.] I know now why Madame was so much agitated when she looked upon my face.

*Mor.* Sir, you are deceived. This is *not* Madame Florentine.

*Col.* Then will Madame oblige me by removing her mask.

*Mor.* You have no right to request it!

*Col.* Then I address myself to you, sir.

*Mor.* Just as you please.

*Enter* LUCENAY, C.

*Col.* And M. Lucernay, here will act as our second.

*Luce.* I, your second. [*Agitated.*] Not I, sir—I am a principal here, Not a second, for I divine the face that is hid behind that mask.

*Mor.* [*Aside.*] What?

*Luce.* The wife of Monsieur Morris on this occasion is *my wife!*

*Col.* No sir it is Madame Florentine.

*Luce.* No sir, it is my wife!

*Mor.* It is neither the one nor the other, but my wife, sir's, as I have said.

*Luce. and Col.* And as we deny.

*Mor.* Dery!

*Both,* Flatly.

*Luce.* I am ready, sir, to support my denial.

*Col.* And, I pray, choose between us.

*Mor.* I won't choose, I will fight both at once, if you like.

[AMELIA *passes between the* COLONEL *and* LUCENAY.

*Luce.* [*To* AMELIA.] This thing shall not end here, Madame. [AMELIA *unmasks and looks in his face.*] Oh, Lord!

*Col.* False woman, never. AMELIA *turns to him.*] Good heavens!

*Luce.* [*Bows to* MORRIS.] Sir, I beg your pardon.

*Col* [*Bowing to* MORRIS.] When one is in the wrong—

*Luce.* The duty of a gentleman—

*Col.* Is to recognise his fault.

*Luce.* And to repair it at once.

*Col.* And in the fullest manner.

*Both.* Pray sir, accept our amplest apologies.

*Mor.* [*Amazed.*] What does it all mean?

*Both.* Let us hope the matter will end here, sir.

*Mor.* Pray inform me gentlemen, what has brought you so suddenly to your senses?

*Both.* Madame. [*Bowing to the* LADY.

LUCENAY *exits by middle dor—the* COLONEL *turns to the same direction and* LAMOURET *appears from* R. H. *door.*

*Lam.* [*Whispers to* MORRIS.] All's right in *there.*

*Col.* There! where!

*Lam.* She's *furious*, and I am to take her away.

*Col.* [*To* LAMOURET.] You are at supper.

*Lam.* Yes, I've won my bet!

*He re-enters his cabinet—the* COLONEL *looks in after him and starts with surprise.*

*Col.* Ah, ha! we shall see. [*Exit*, L.

*Ame.* Well now, sir, that we are alone—

*Mor.* Now that we are alone and I saved by a miracle from two duels I have to say to you Madame Florentine, that am your servant and that I renounce you forever.

*Ame.* [*Repressing her satisfaction.*] Can it be?

*Mor.* Yes, Madame, think what you like of me, and of American gallantry. You shan't complain, at least of American honesty. I shall never see you again.

*Ame.* Sir, you don't so easily get rid of me.

*Mor.* But I tell you, Madame, I mean to go home at once.

*Ame.* Very well, then I'll go with you.

*Mor.* Madame, you forget that I am a married man. I admit that I don't behave like one, but it is true, and my wife is the best of women, and the loveliest.

*Ame.* [*Ironically.*] Ah!

*Mor.* Yes, Madame—and I love her—and I alwas have loved her—and I've played the fool and the mule long enough, but I will try and make amends to her, for a faul. of which she knows nothing.

*Amr.* But of which she she shall know everything, and from me.

*Mor.* Merciful heaven, are you my evil genius! Why did I ever come to Paris.

*Ame.* I will tell her all.

*Mor.* [*Falls on his knees.*] I intreat—I implore you. She is not a French woman—she does not believe all men deceivers by nature—she trusts me. In heaven's name, do not destroy her confidence in me now, when I am resolved to deserve it.

*Ame.* I will tell it all; I *have* told all; she knows all!

[*Takes off her mask.*

*Mor.* Amelia! My wife! [*He tries to rise.*

*Ame.* [*Preventing him.*] No, stay where yon are—where you *ought to be*.. Ah! you have been guilty, very guilty.

*Mor.* Yes, yes, I have, and I own it, and as senseless as I have been guilty.

*Ame.* [*Looks at him and smiles.*] I know how you have been tempted—how you have been misled. You are not a *very* bad creature, though after all; and I now believe you do love me, that love does xcuse.

*Mor.* Everything?

*Ame.* *Something!*

*Mor.* Ah, yes. My wife, my dear, dear wife.

*Ame.* Yes, your dear wife, who has saved you from—

*Enter* BOTHERER, L., *does not see* AMELIA.

*Both.* Morris, vou are lost!

*Mor.* Eh? how so?

*Both.* I found a cab at last, get your wife into it—

*Mor. My wife!*

*Both.* Yes, your wife who was then in that cabinet, and I have driven back, still leaving my hospital, to tell you she knows all.

*Ame.* [*Comes forward.*] And she pardons all!

*Both.* [*Amazed.*] Ah! together. Well Madame, do I no sooner get you in the cab, than off you come again.

*Ame.* [*Aside.*] Annie is safe. He never recognised her.

*Both.* Now you are in blue, just now you were in black. Who the deuce did I put in my cab? *Exit,* L. 3 E.

*Ame.* 'Tis Annie, I changed dominoes with her.

*Mor.* Annie! It's all right. Ha! ha! ha! I can't help laughing at the doctor's amazement as he discovers her in the cab.

*Enter* BOTHERER *and* ANNIE.

*Both.* My dear Annie, why do I find you here? *You* surely did not come here to meet your *broker?* [*Looking at Morris.*] I'm afraid you are on a bender, as they say in New York.

*Annie.* My dear husband I will tell you. From a few words of Amelia's, which I accidentally overheard, I suspected that she was going to the Opera Ball in pursuit of her husband; and—and—feeling much alarmed for her safety, I was induced to accept Madame Giraud's invitation to accompany her to the ball, where I was fortunate enough to find Amelia, and you, my dear husband. [*They embrace.*

*Both.* Well my dear Annie, I am glad you are here, here are our friends, and since virtue is triumphant, I'll put you in your carriage and be off to the Hospital; and as they say in New York, "never go on a bender again." Now, then friends, since virtue is triumphant, I'll just put you in your carriage and be off to the Hospital. Up with your coat collar *for the last time*, let us hope in your life. [*To* MR MORRIS.] And now come.

*Enter* LAMOURET.

*Lam.* Huzza! huzza! She is perfectly fascinated. I shall win my wager, and now my friend, the Colonel, perhaps.

*Both.* Oh, by the bye, Lamouret, that reminds me I have a message for you.

*Lam.* I trust it's not from a lady, doctor, for really—just now—

*Both.* Oh! bless you, do. It's from Colonel de Sabres.

*Lam.* Ah, ha!

*Both.* Yes. He says you'll thoroughly comprehend it. First, I'm to ask you what your chance is of winning your wager.

*Lam.* Capital—excellent—all but certain.

*Both.* Exactly—then I'm to tell you emphatically that he is waiting for you, and that his carriage is at your service.

*Lam. Aghast!* Run—eh—yes—she is—I wish you all good evening. [*Exit hastily.*

*Enter* DE SABRES, L. H., *crosses to* R., *and exit—Then* LUCENAY *same business.*

*Both* Now what the deuce is the matter with him? However, I've given my message, so come let us be off, we are about the only peo ple left here, I think.

*Mor.* Not exactly. Here are a few that it would be as well, per haps, to bid farewell to.

*Both.* Oh, by the bye, yes, to be sure. Ladies and gentlemen, have seen us safely through our several entanglements, and we respectfully bid you good-night. If, however, my services will, in your opinion, be of any avail to any of you, I shall at all times, be happy to return. And, if *I* am not always on the spot, there are partners of mine, who have practised with me for some years, who will do the best for your case. One thing I must mention: don't send for me in cases of neuralgia or headache, because it is very clear that one of my partners understands those complaints much more thoroughly than I do. In the meantime, as the remedy for ennui and low spirits which you have so kindly taken to-night is it's composer's first mixture, pray allow the old practitioner to recommend the young beginner to your best indulgence and consideration.

THE END.

www.ingramcontent.com/pod-product-compliance
Lightning Source LLC
LaVergne TN
LVHW020741120826
845150LV00010B/2292

* 9 7 8 1 4 1 8 1 9 3 9 2 8 *